Draw a picture or
place a photograph
of yourself here.

This book belongs to:

_____

Meet Marvin the Magician. He lives
in a castle hidden deep in the
mountains. He carries his magic
staff with him at all times—in case
there is any trouble.

As Marvin is researching some new magic spells, a pigeon arrives with a message. Can you help the pigeon navigate through the shelves and reach Marvin?

maze craze
Magician's Castle

Sterling Publishing Co., Inc.
New York

Published in 2005 by Sterling Publishing Co., Inc.
387 Park Avenue South, New York, NY 10016
Originally published in Germany under the title
Zauberduell im Drachenschloss by Edition Bücherbär im Arena Verlag GmbH
Copyright © 2005 by Edition Bücherbär im Arena Verlag GmbH
English Translation by Daniel Shea
English Translation Copyright © 2005 by Sterling Publishing Co., Inc.
Distributed in Canada by Sterling Publishing
C/o Canadian Manda Group, 165 Dufferin Street
Toronto, Ontario, Canada M6K 3H6
Distributed in Great Britain and Europe by Chris Lloyd at Orca Book Services
Stanley House, Fleets Lane, Poole BH15 3AJ, England
Distributed in Australia by Capricorn Link (Australia) Pty Ltd.
P.O. Box 704, Windsor, NSW 2756, Australia

For information about custom editions, special sales, premium and
corporate purchases, please contact Sterling Special Sales
Department at 800-805-5489 or specialsales@sterlingpub.com.

Manufactured in China
All Rights Reserved

Sterling ISBN 1-4027-2652-X

10 9 8 7 6 5 4

Marvin quickly unfolds the note and reads the urgent message:

Help, Marvin! I've been kidnapped by the evil sorcerer, Furor. I'm locked in the Dragon Castle. Please come quickly!

Princess Lacrima

Start

End

"I have to save Princess Lacrima!" exclaims Marvin. He looks at his map to see where the Dragon Castle is located. How can he reach it on the map by moving ONLY over the red dragons?

Marvin grabs his magic staff and runs down the steps as fast as he can.

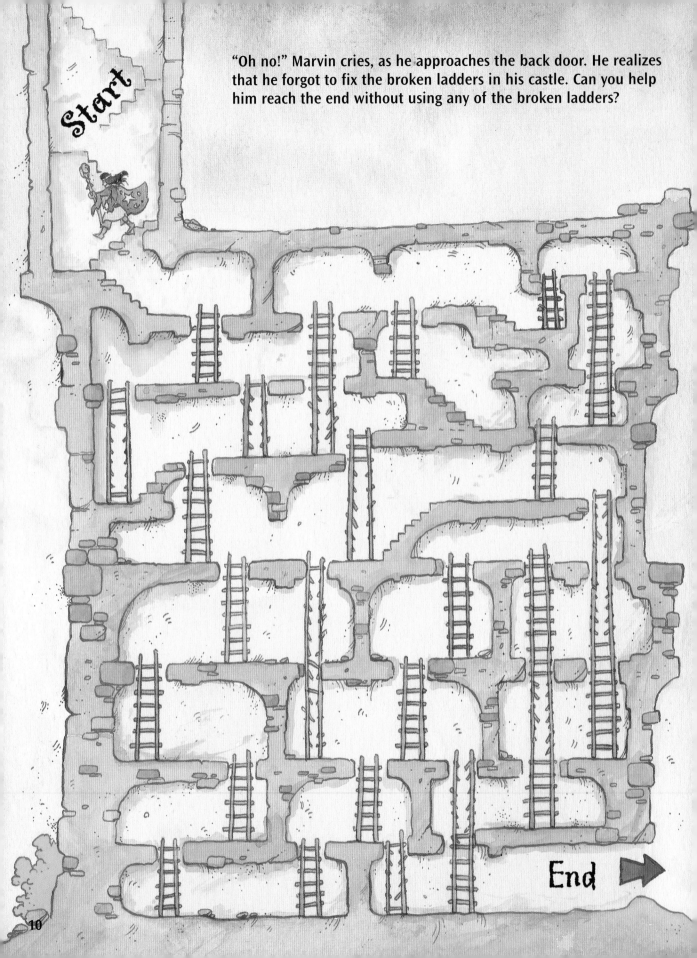

"Oh no!" Marvin cries, as he approaches the back door. He realizes that he forgot to fix the broken ladders in his castle. Can you help him reach the end without using any of the broken ladders?

Finally he reaches the back garden. Can you help him find his way out of the hedges?

End

Marvin enters the Lost Forest, where many people have gotten lost in the winding paths. Marvin casts a spell and places arrows to lead him to the end. How can he reach the end without walking against the direction in which the arrows point?

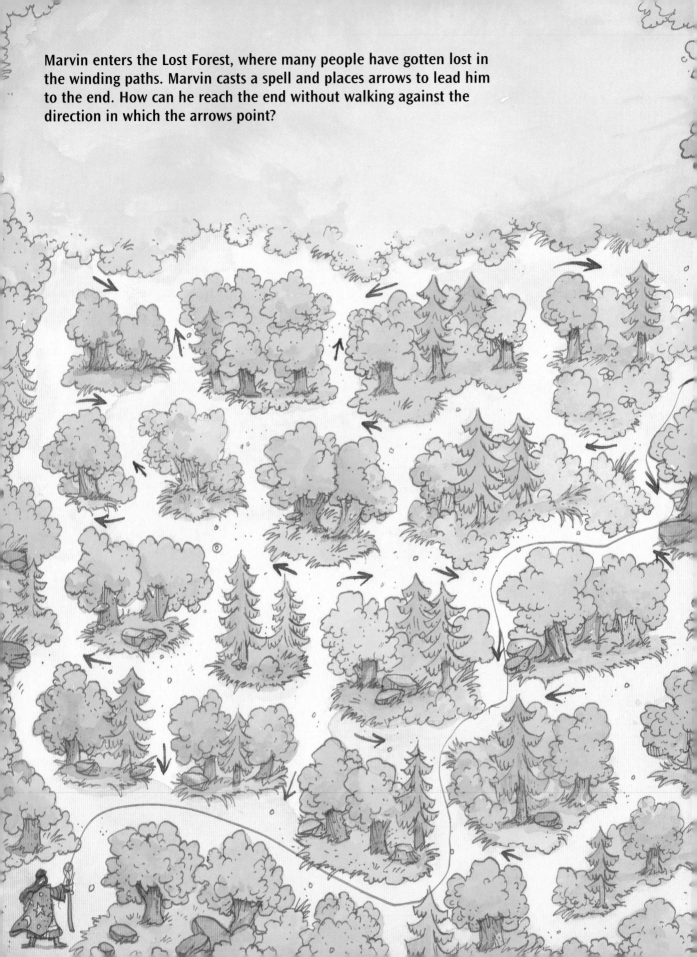

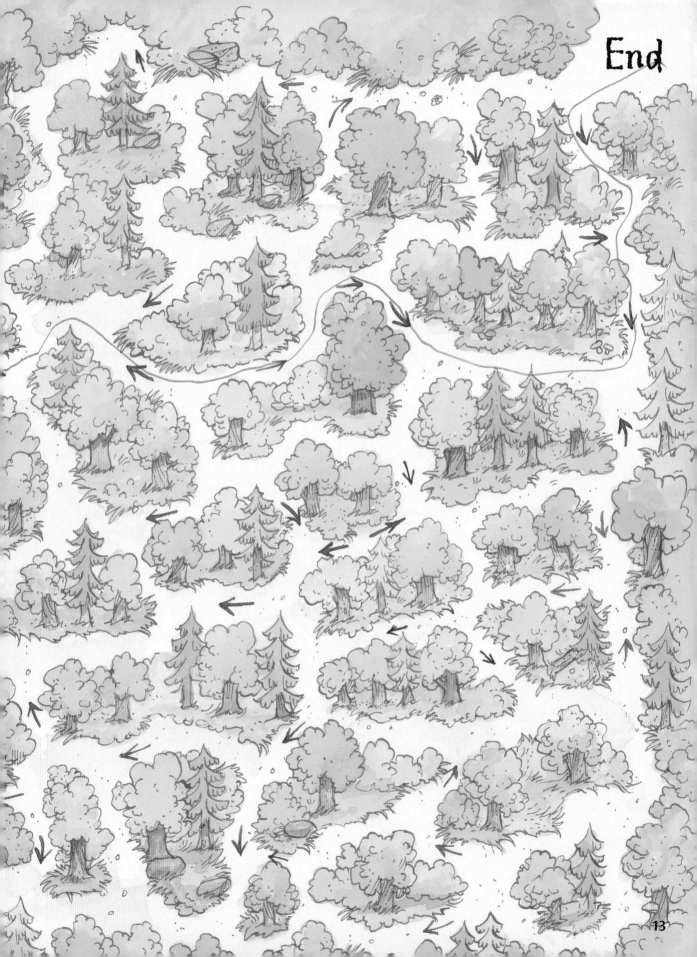

End

13

Marvin suddenly encounters a white unicorn. "I will let you pass only if you correctly solve this maze," the unicorn tells him. How can Marvin reach the end by using only the shields with the colors red and blue?

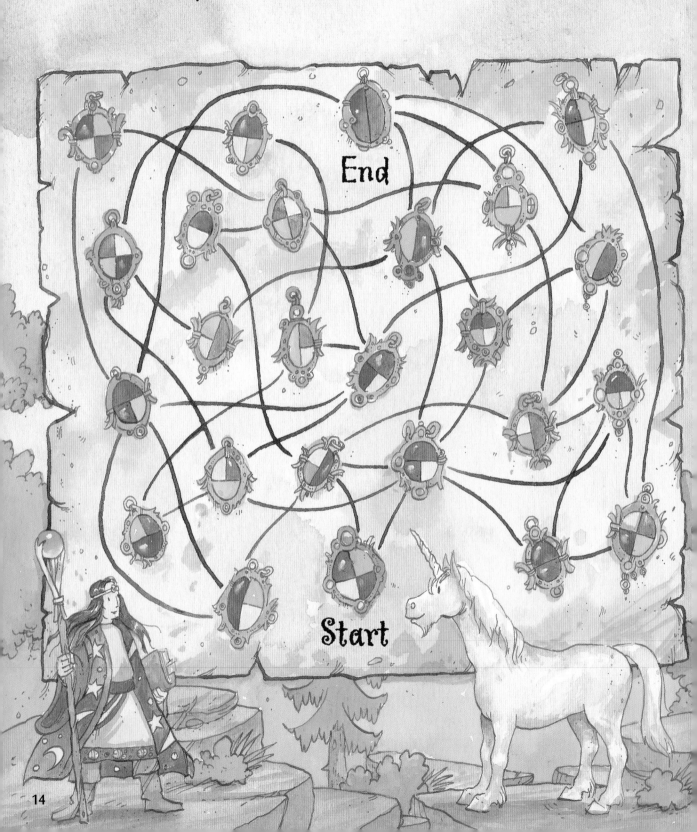

End

Start

Marvin meets his friend Billy the Farmer. "Don't step on any of my precious mushrooms!" Billy yells to Marvin.

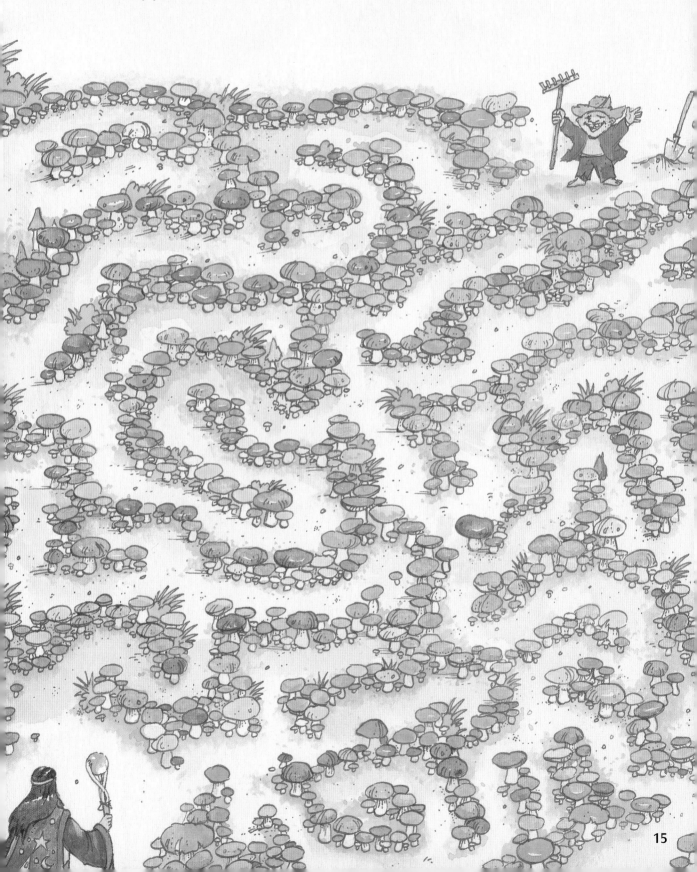

Marvin passes his friend Zelda's house. "Maybe she knows the way to the Dragon Castle," he thinks to himself. Unfortunately, Zelda isn't home.

End

Marvin suddenly hears voices coming from the ground. Marvin is relieved when he discovers that they are from his friends Earl and Thomas, who are miners. He asks them if they know the way to the Dragon Castle. "We can't hear you!" they shout. "Come down here, but only use numbers that add up to 266!"

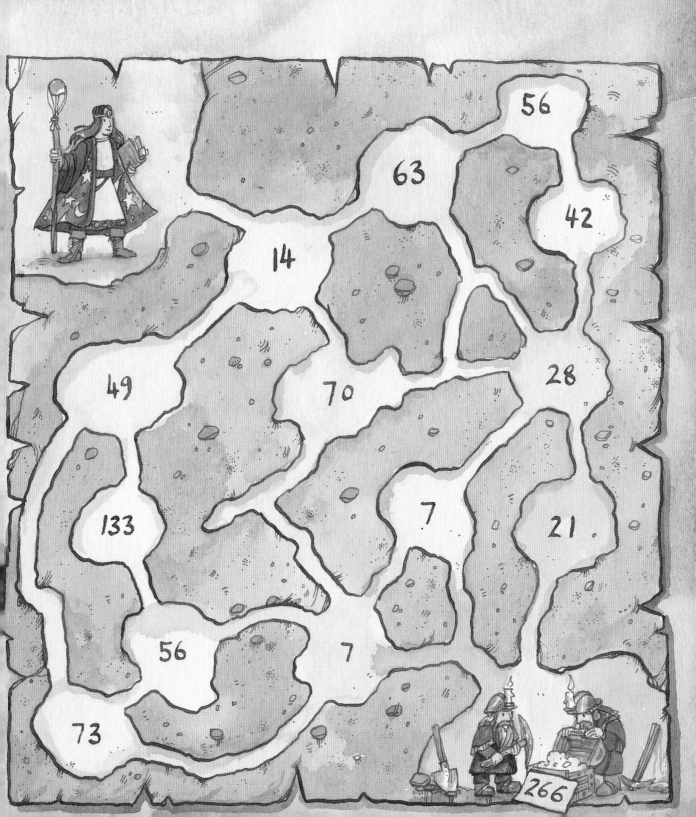

Marvin sees Myra the Mermaid. "Do you know the way to the Dragon Castle?" he asks. "I'm sorry, but I don't. Could you help me untangle my pet goldfish from the plants though?" she asks him.

End

Start

"I bet Garry the Gnome will know the way to the Dragon Castle!" Marvin says.
How can Marvin reach Garry by moving only in the direction of the arrows?

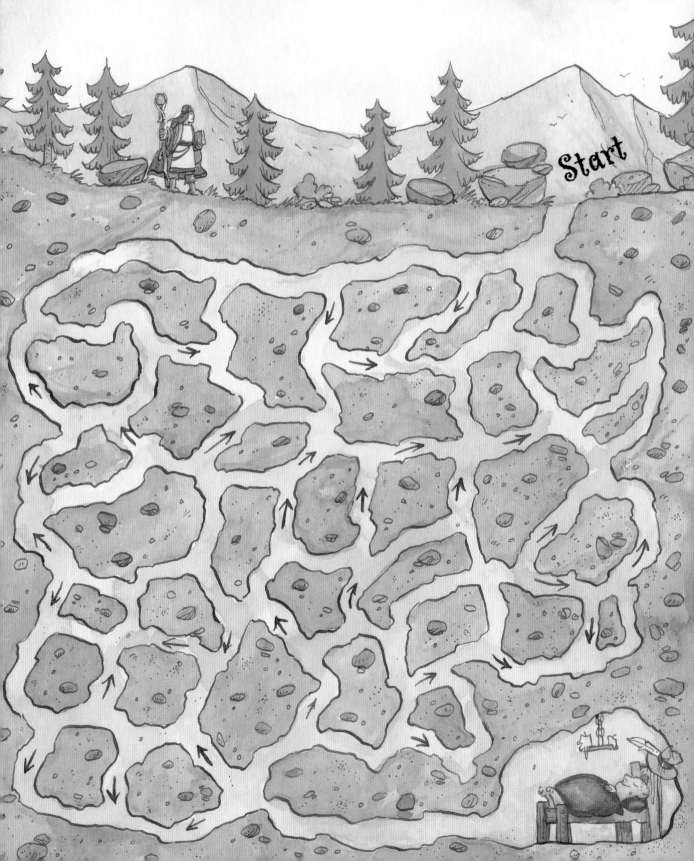

Garry tells Marvin that Vlad the Vampire knows the fastest way to the Dragon Castle. However, in order to find Vlad, Marvin has to find his way through a town of clay houses. Can you help Marvin move through the ladders?

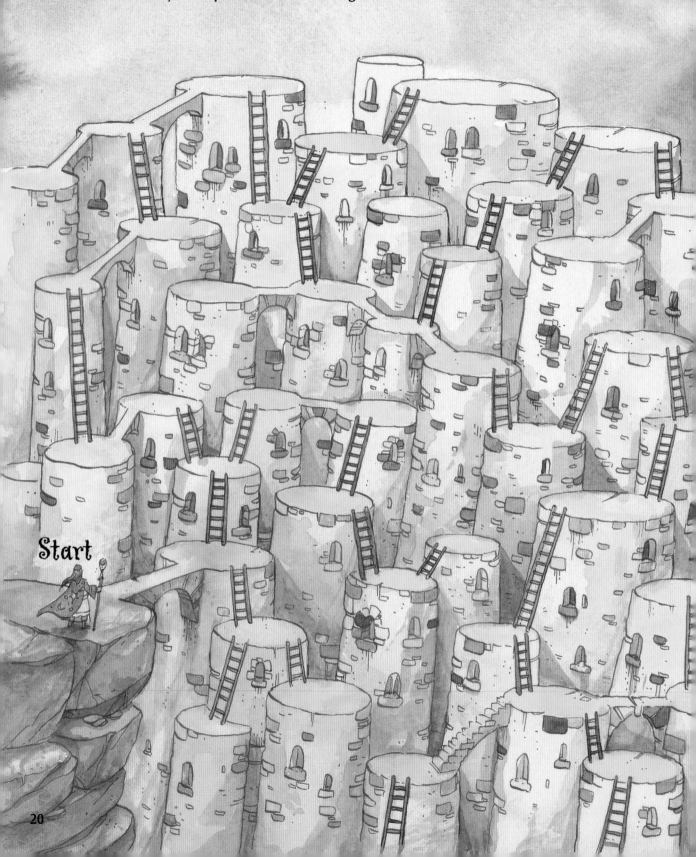

Start

End

Marvin finds Vlad, but can only reach him through the messy maze.

"You first have to climb over a cliff in order to reach the Dragon Castle. Allow only the red-winged bats to help you climb the rocks," Vlad tells Marvin.

End

Start

Uh Oh! Marvin is lost again. Maybe Twyla the Fairy can help him.

Marvin is back on track, and soon approaches a bridge. "I will only let you cross this bridge if you solve the maze," the black knight tells Marvin.

Start

End

Finally, Marvin sees the Dragon Castle in the distance! In order to reach it, he must first cross the ancient ruins without using any of the broken ladders.

End

27

Can you help Marvin cross the marsh?

End

When Marvin enters the Dragon Castle, the evil sorcerer Furor is waiting for him. "You'll never rescue Princess Lacrima without a fight!" he roars. What's the fastest way for Marvin to meet Furor?

Start

End

Marvin defeats Furor, but where is the key to Princess Lacrima's cell?
Which rope does Marvin have to use?

"We need to get out of here as fast as possible!" Marvin tells Princess Lacrima. How can they reach Marvin's castle without running into any wolves?

Marvin returns the Princess to her home. Princess Lacrima's father, King Edward, thanks Marvin by throwing a huge celebration in his honor.

Start

End

Answers

page 6

page 7

page 8

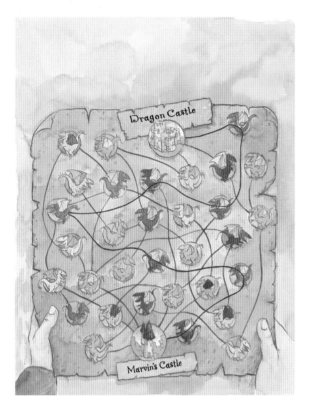

page 9

page 10

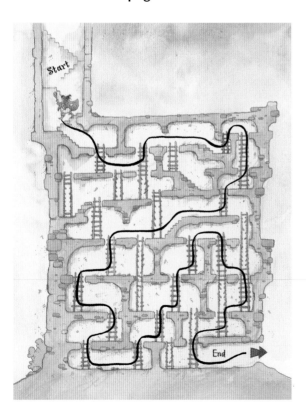

page 11

pages 12–13

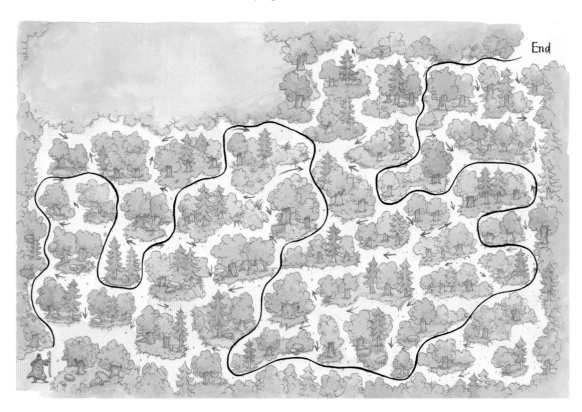

End

page 14

End

Start

page 15

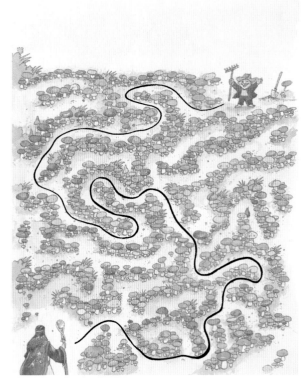

End

page 16

page 17

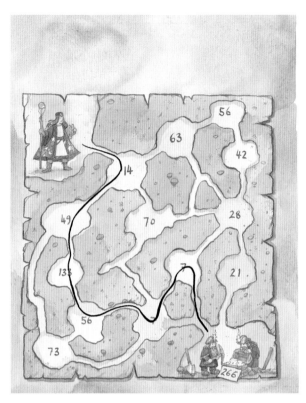

page 18

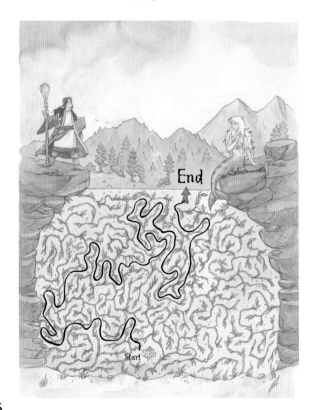

page 19

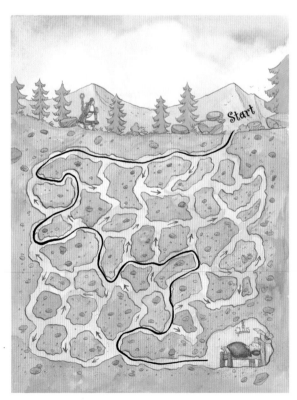

pages 20–21

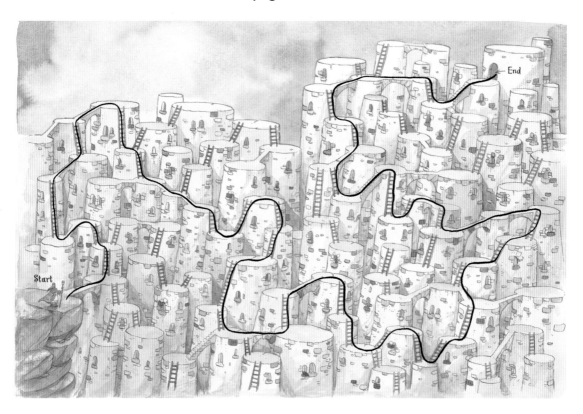

page 22

page 23

pages 26–27

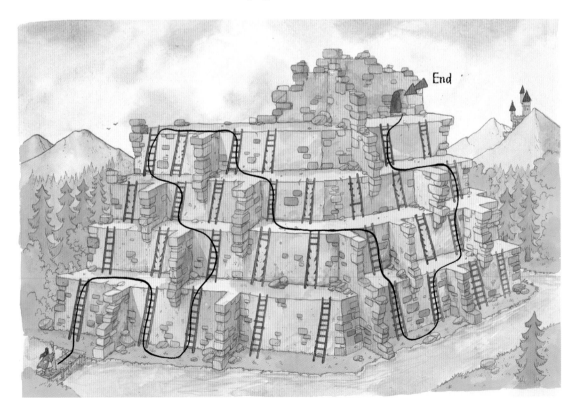

page 28

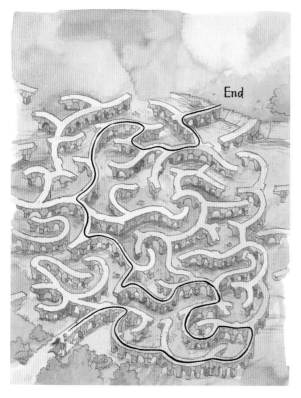

page 29

page 30

The key is hanging on rope C.

(The sword is on rope B; the book is on rope D;
and the hourglass is on rope A.)

page 31